Math Mammoth Grade 2
Skills Review Workbook
Answer Key

By Maria Miller

Copyright 2017-2023 Taina Maria Miller
ISBN 978-1-942715-30-6

2017 Edition

All rights reserved. No part of this book may be reproduced or transmitted in any form or by any means, electronic or mechanical, or by any information storage and retrieval system, without permission in writing from the author.

Copying permission: For having purchased this book, the copyright owner grants to the teacher-purchaser a limited permission to reproduce this material for use with his or her students. In other words, the teacher-purchaser MAY make copies of the pages, or an electronic copy of the PDF file, and provide them at no cost to the students he or she is actually teaching, but not to students of other teachers. This permission also extends to the spouse of the purchaser, for the purpose of providing copies for the children in the same family. Sharing the file with anyone else, whether via the Internet or other media, is strictly prohibited.

No permission is granted for resale of the material.

The copyright holder also grants permission to the purchaser to make electronic copies of the material for back-up purposes.

If you have other needs, such as licensing for a school or tutoring center, please contact the author at https://www.MathMammoth.com/contact

Contents

	Work-text page	Answer key page
Chapter 1: Some Old, Some New		
Skills Review 1	7	5
Skills Review 2	8	5
Skills Review 3	9	5
Skills Review 4	10	6
Skills Review 5	11	6
Skills Review 6	12	6
Skills Review 7	13	7
Skills Review 8	14	7
Skills Review 9	15	7
Chapter 2: Clock		
Skills Review 10	16	8
Skills Review 11	17	8
Skills Review 12	18	9
Skills Review 13	19	9
Skills Review 14	20	9
Skills Review 15	21	10
Skills Review 16	22	10
Skills Review 17	23	10
Chapter 3: Addition and Subtraction Facts Within 0-18		
Skills Review 18	24	11
Skills Review 19	25	11
Skills Review 20	26	11
Skills Review 21	27	12
Skills Review 22	28	12
Skills Review 23	29	13
Skills Review 24	30	13
Skills Review 25	31	13
Skills Review 26	32	14
Skills Review 27	33	14
Skills Review 28	34	15
Skills Review 29	35	15
Skills Review 30	36	16
Skills Review 31	37	16
Skills Review 32	38	17
Skills Review 33	39	17
Skills Review 34	40	17
Chapter 4: Regrouping in Addition		
Skills Review 35	41	18
Skills Review 36	42	18
Skills Review 37	43	18
Skills Review 38	44	19
Skills Review 39	45	19
Skills Review 40	46	19
Skills Review 41	47	20
Skills Review 42	48	20
Skills Review 43	49	20
Chapter 5: Geometry and Fractions		
Skills Review 44	50	21
Skills Review 45	51	21
Skills Review 46	52	21
Skills Review 47	53	22
Skills Review 48	54	22
Skills Review 49	55	22
Skills Review 50	56	22
Skills Review 51	57	23
Chapter 6: Three-Digit Numbers		
Skills Review 52	58	24
Skills Review 53	59	24
Skills Review 54	60	24
Skills Review 55	61	25
Skills Review 56	62	25
Skills Review 57	63	26
Skills Review 58	64	26
Skills Review 59	65	26
Chapter 7: Measuring		
Skills Review 60	66	27
Skills Review 61	67	27
Skills Review 62	68	27
Skills Review 63	69	27
Skills Review 64	70	28
Skills Review 65	71	28
Skills Review 66	72	28
Skills Review 67	73	28

	Work-text page	Answer key page

Chapter 8: Regrouping in Addition and Subtraction

Skills Review 68	74	29
Skills Review 69	75	29
Skills Review 70	76	29
Skills Review 71	77	30
Skills Review 72	78	30
Skills Review 73	79	30
Skills Review 74	80	31
Skills Review 75	81	31
Skills Review 76	82	31

Chapter 9: Money

Skills Review 77	83	32
Skills Review 78	84	32
Skills Review 79	85	32
Skills Review 80	86	33
Skills Review 81	87	33

Chapter 10: Exploring Multiplication

Skills Review 82	88	34
Skills Review 83	89	34
Skills Review 84	90	34
Skills Review 85	91	34

Chapter 1: Some Old, Some New

Skills Review 1, p. 7

1.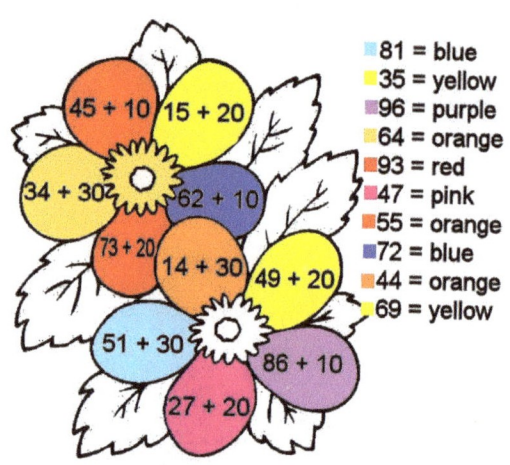

2. a. 22   b. 31   c. 32

3. a. 33 + 4 + 3 = 40. Becky gave her 3 stickers.
   b. She has 20 stickers left.

4. a. 45   b. 13   c. 25   d. 43

Skills Review 2, p. 8

1. a. 86, 84, 82, 80, 78, 76, 74, 72, 70, 68   b. 105, 95, 85, 75, 65, 55, 45, 35, 25, 15

2. a. 8   b. 10   c. 11

3. a. He found five fewer pine cones.   b. They found 29 pine cones.

4. a. 0   b. 38   c. 49   d. 15

5. a. 3, 6, 9   3 + 6 = 9; 6 + 3 = 9; 9 − 6 = 3; 9 − 3 = 6
   b. 30, 50, 80   30 + 50 = 80; 50 + 30 = 80; 80 − 50 = 30; 80 − 30 = 50

Skills Review 3, p. 9

1.
13	+	30	=	43
+				
20	+	56	=	76
=		−		−
33		30		40
		=		=
10	+	26	=	36

2. a. 34   b. 86   c. 98   d. 21

3.
7 + 3 = 10   4 + 5 = 9   10 − 2 = 8
6 − 4 = 2   10 − 8 = 2   5 + 4 = 9
9 − 5 = 4   2 + 4 = 6   10 − 7 = 3
8 + 2 = 10   3 + 7 = 10   6 − 2 = 4

4. a. 30 + 20 + 25 = 75; They picked 75 oranges.
   b. 30 + 18 = 48; She still needs to make 18 more cupcakes.
      Now she needs to make 8 more cupcakes.

Skills Review 4, p. 10

1.

2.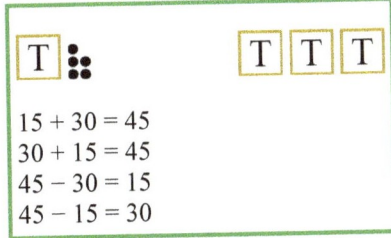

$15 + 30 = 45$
$30 + 15 = 45$
$45 - 30 = 15$
$45 - 15 = 30$

3. a. She gathered 30 eggs.
   b. He has $51 left. He needs $3 more dollars to buy the camera.

4. a. 42, 44, 46, 48, 50, 52, 54, 56, 58
   b. 105, 100, 95, 90, 85, 80, 75, 70, 65

Skills Review 5, p. 11

1. a. yes, even   b. no, odd   c. no, odd

2. a. 10   b. 18   c. 3   d. 3

3. a. She caught five more fireflies. No, he caught one fewer.

4. They each got seven muffins.

5. a. fifth from the left   b. second from the right
   c. ninth from the right   d. seventh from the left

Skills Review 6, p. 12

1. a. 24   b. 46   c. 88   d. 62

2.

Balloons	Even	Odd
18	E	
7		O
11		O

Balloons	Even	Odd
5		O
12	E	
14	E	

3. Each girl got 15 flowers.

4. Adrian ate 5 pancakes.

5. a. 5   b. 30   c. 6   d. 7

Skills Review 7, p. 13

1. Baked

2. a. 6 + 24 = 30; 30 − 6 = 24   b. 8 + 8 = 16; 16 − 8 = 8

3. 18, 20, 22, 24, 26, 28, 30

4.
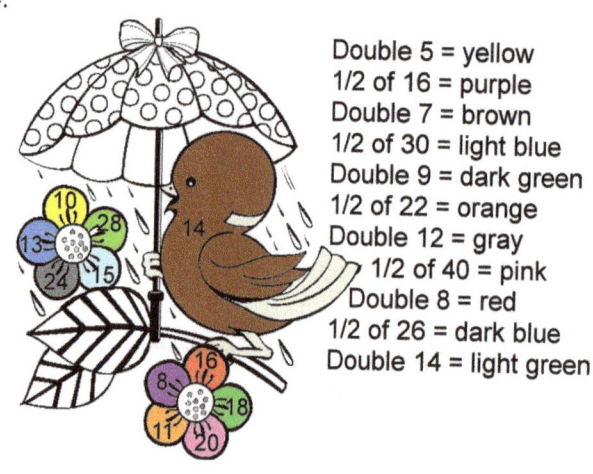

5. 3, 5, 7, 9, 11, 13, 15, 17, 19, 21, 23, 25, 27

Skills Review 8, p. 14

1. a. 30   b. 6

2. ODD (BLUE) 15, 5, 13, 11, 7, 9, 1, 3
   EVEN (RED) 2, 6, 14, 4, 16, 10, 12, 8

3. a. 10 + 10   b. 7 + 7   c. 15 + 15   d. 6 + 6

4. a. She has a total of 37 students in her class; 32 students came to school.
   b. Each boy would get 20 strawberries.
      There are 35 strawberries left and they cannot be shared equally.
   c. She has 15 more coins.

Skills Review 9, p. 15

1. There are other correct answers for a, b, c, and e. The pictures below give just one possible answer.

a.   b.   c.   d.   e.

2. She has five more colored pencils. Kayla now has 18 colored pencils and that is an even number.

3.
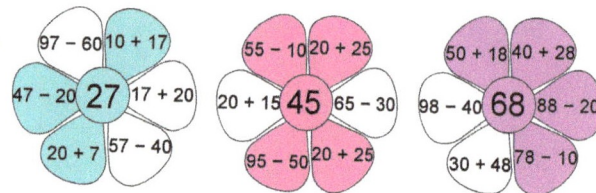

4. a. 66   b. 24   c. 42   d. 88

Chapter 2: Clock

Skills Review 10, p. 16

1. a. 8 o'clock; 8:00   b. half past 2; 2:30
2. 7 + 4 = 11; 4 + 7 = 11; 11 − 7 = 4; 11 − 4 = 7
3. a. 20   b. 1/2 of 60 is 30   c. 1/2 of 24 is 12
4. a. He had $29 left.   b. Now he has $79.
5.

7	12	17	22	27	32	37	42	47	52	57	62	67
11	16	21	26	31	36	41	46	51	56	61	66	71

Skills Review 11, p. 17

1.

2. a. 9:30   b. 3:00
3. a. 1:00   b. 9:30
4. a. 33   b. 87   c. 23   d. 87

Puzzle corner: The answers will vary. Please check the student's answers.

20	+	30	+	10	=	60
+		+		+		
30	+	30	+	30	=	90
+		+		+		
50	+	10	+	10	=	70
=		=		=		
100		70		50		

10	+	20	+	30	=	60
+		+		+		
40	+	40	+	10	=	90
+		+		+		
50	+	10	+	10	=	70
=		=		=		
100		70		50		

20	+	20	+	20	=	60
+		+		+		
50	+	30	+	10	=	90
+		+		+		
30	+	20	+	20	=	70
=		=		=		
100		70		50		

40	+	10	+	10	=	60
+		+		+		
40	+	40	+	10	=	90
+		+		+		
20	+	20	+	30	=	70
=		=		=		
100		70		50		

Skills Review 12, p. 18

1. a. 6; 19 − 6 = 13
   b. 8; 90 − 8 = 82

2. Please check the student's answers. The answers will vary.
   For example: 66 − ____ = 32 or ____ + 55 = 72

3. a. The children finished playing tag at 6:30.
      They ate supper at 7:00.
   b. Each boy will get $12.
   c. Mom needs to buy 14 notebooks.

4. a. 1:35   b. 4:05   c. 2:55   d. 7:15

Skills Review 13, p. 19

1. a. 16   b. 80   c. 16   d. 50

2. a. 6:40; 6:45   b. 11:10; 11:15

3. a. 60   b. 79   c. 73

4. Megan has 8 crayons left.

5. He found 15 toy cars.
   No, 15 is not an even number.

6.

a. The fourth frog from the left.   b. The second duck from the right.

Skills Review 14, p. 20

1 - 2.

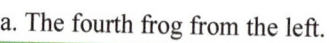

3. They planted a total of 77 flower seeds. Fifty-two seeds did not sprout.

4. The meatloaf will be done at 5:30. Dad got home at 6:00.

5.

a. It is 35 minutes till 3 o'clock.
b. It is 15 minutes till 8 o'clock.
c. It is 40 minutes till 1 o'clock.
d. It is 5 minutes till 4 o'clock.

Skills Review 15, p. 21

1. Sunflowers

2. They spent five hours in the park.

3. They finished cleaning the house at 10:00.

4.

a.			b.			c.			d.		
	1	3		9	6		4	3		8	7
+	1	3	−	4	4	+	5	4	−	4	6
	2	6		5	2		9	7		4	1

5. a. 1:15   b. 5:25   c. 12:20   d. 2:50

Skills Review 16, p. 22

1.

a.	b.	c.
6 + 6 = 12	25 + 25 = 50	18 + 18 = 36
$\frac{1}{2}$ of 12 is 6.	$\frac{1}{2}$ of 50 is 25.	$\frac{1}{2}$ of 36 is 18.

2. May, June, July
   August, September, October

3. Each boy will get 23 marbles. They have 38 marbles left.
   They can share them equally because 38 is an even number.

4. She had 32 cookies left.

5. 6 hours,   11 hours,   6 hours,   21 hours,   16 hours

Skills Review 17, p. 23

1. a. One week ago it was August 5th.
   b. It is August 26th.

2.

a. + 20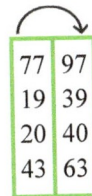

b. − 10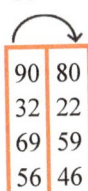

c. + 5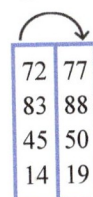

3. She has 40 items. Now she has 60 items to treasure.

4. August 10th is Wednesday. August 27th is Saturday.

5. a. 12:05   b. 8:40   c. 6:10   d. 2:30

Chapter 3: Addition and Subtraction Facts Within 0-18

Skills Review 18, p. 24

1.

+10		+20		+30		+40	
36	46	71	91	44	74	29	69
E	E	O	O	E	E	O	O

2. 7:30   12:00   1:15   10:00

3.

a.	4	2	b.	7	9	c.	3	6	d.	7	5
+	4	7	−	5	3	+	4	2	−	4	3
	8	9		2	6		7	8		3	2

4. He stayed four hours.

5. Seven of the children were boys.

6. a. 69, 59   b. 12, 2   c. 55, 35

Skills Review 19, p. 25

1.

30	33	36	39	42	45	48	51	54	57
26	29	32	35	38	41	44	47	50	53

2. She put 48 items in the wrong places.

3. Her grandma is coming March 28th. Her grandma did not come until April 4th.

4. a. 4   b. 42 + 8 = 50   c. 74 + 6 = 80

5. a. 1 o'clock, 1:00   b. half past 7, 7:30   c. half past 3, 3:30   d. 11 o'clock, 11:00

Skills Review 20, p. 26

1. a. Friday   b. Wednesday   c. Tuesday   d. Sunday

2. a. 13   b. 16   c. 14

3. a. 5   b. 4   c. 3

4. a. They each got 12 watermelons.
   b. Together, they have $45.
   c. There were 24 cherries left in the basket.

5. a. 6   b. 9   c. 3

Skills Review 21, p. 27

1.

   ART   TOM   DON   SID   RAY   BOB   JIM   MAX

2.

9	+	5	=	14
+				
8	+	3	=	11
=		+		+
17		9		9
		=		=
8	+	12	=	20

3. She needs 7 more apples.
   Mom had 8 apples left over.

4. He finished washing the car at 5 o'clock.

5. a. half past 1
   b. 10 till 8
   c. 25 past 11

Skills Review 22, p. 28

1.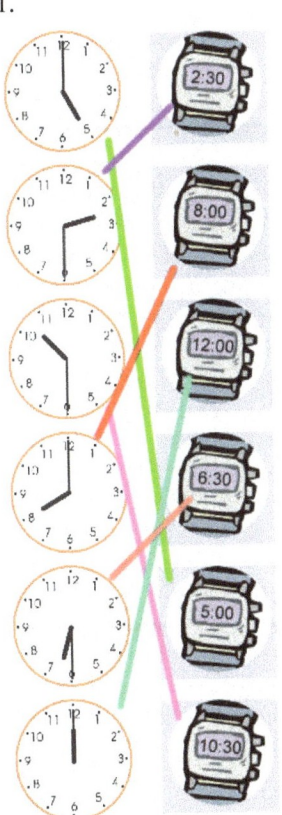

2. a. 2, 3, 4   b. 4, 5, 6

3. He visited her in January.

4. She went shopping September 12th.

5.

12	19	26	33	40	47	54	61	68	75	82	89	96
3	10	17	24	31	38	45	52	59	66	73	80	87

Skills Review 23, p. 29

1. a. 30   b. 25
   c. 60   d. 47

2. He found his homework on Monday.

3. They are going to visit Hawaii in July.

4.

11 = brown
12 = gray
13 = pink
14 = red
15 = yellow
16 = blue
17 = green
18 = orange
19 = purple

5. 14 hours, 6 hours, 12 hours, 10 hours, 13 hours

Skills Review 24, p. 30

1.

8 + 0 = 8	8 + 5 = 13	8 + 8 = 16	8 + 9 = 17
8 + 3 = 11	8 + 7 = 15	8 + 1 = 9	8 + 4 = 12
8 + 10 = 18	8 + 1 = 9	8 + 6 = 14	8 + 2 = 10

2. Each one had 9 roses.

3. a. 4   b. 3   c. 3

4. a. 33   b. 41   c. 33   d. 14

5. a. 4:45, 4:50   b. 7:20, 7:25   c. 12:05, 12:10   d. 1:25, 1:30

Skills Review 25, p. 31

1. She will bake bread on March 4th, 11th, 18th, and 25th.

2.

7	12	9	5	4
11	18	10	14	6
27	15	11	19	16
22	36	20	18	21
23	26	45	27	24
29	31	54	63	32
36	23	39	37	72
42	49	43	81	46
49	41	90	48	42
53	99	47	56	51

3. a. 11, 8, 9   b. 6, 7, 9

4. a. She sold 8 puppies.   b. He will leave at 7.

Skills Review 26, p. 32

1.

9 + 0 = 9	9 + 5 = 14	9 + 9 = 18	9 + 4 = 13
9 + 3 = 12	9 + 6 = 15	9 + 1 = 10	9 + 10 = 19
9 + 7 = 16	9 + 8 = 17	9 + 2 = 11	

2. 3, 4, 5, 6, 7, 8, 9, 10, 11, 12, 13, 14, 15

3. a. 25 till 5, 5:35   b. 10 past 3, 3:10   c. 20 past 12, 12:20

Puzzle Corner: Please check the student's answers. Answers will vary.

```
 50 + 30 = 80        80 − 30 = 50
  −    −              +    +
 20 + 10 = 30        20 − 0 = 20
  =    =              =    =
 30   20             100   30

 40 + 40 = 80        60 − 10 = 50
  −    −              +    +
 10 + 20 = 30        40 − 20 = 20
  =    =              =    =
 30   20             100   30
```

Skills Review 27, p. 33

1.

a. 14 − 8	b. 13 − 6	c. 17 − 9
/ \	/ \	/ \
14 − 4 − 4 = 6	13 − 3 − 3 = 7	17 − 7 − 2 = 8

2. She needs 7 more popsicle sticks. She has 57 popsicle sticks.

3. He needs 3 more goldfish.

4. a. 14, 15   b. 12, 13   c. 18, 19

5. a. 80, 88, 90; 90 is nearer.   b. 30, 34, 40; 30 is nearer.   c. 20, 21, 30; 20 is nearer.

6. 9 hours, 4 hours, 12 hours, 18 hours, 22 hours

Skills Review 28, p. 34

1.

6 + 0 = 6	6 + 5 = 11	6 + 9 = 15	6 + 6 = 12
6 + 3 = 9	6 + 7 = 13	6 + 4 = 10	6 + 8 = 14
6 + 10 = 16	6 + 1 = 7	6 + 2 = 8	

2. a. 9   b. 8 + 8

3. a. 5   b. 40   c. 5

4. There are 37 blackberries left in his hat. Now, he has 87 blackberries in his hat.

5.

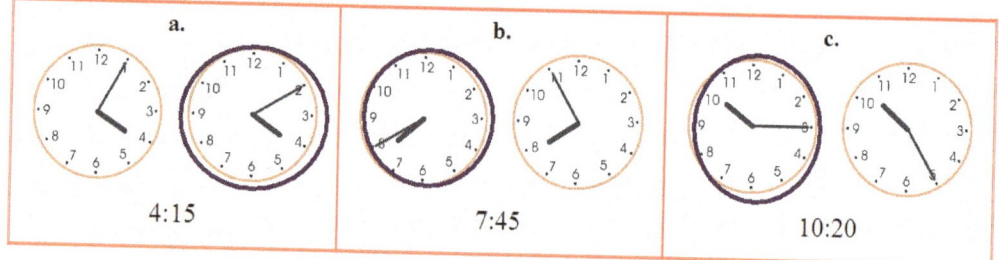

a. 4:15   b. 7:45   c. 10:20

Skills Review 29, p. 35

1.

11 − 4 = 7	11 − 2 = 9	11 − 3 = 8	11 − 9 = 2
11 − 8 = 3	11 − 5 = 6	11 − 6 = 5	11 − 7 = 4

2.

3. 20 oranges   24 peaches   25 plums

Skills Review 30, p. 36

1.

7 + 0 = 7	7 + 5 = 12	7 + 6 = 13	7 + 9 = 16
7 + 3 = 10	7 + 9 = 16	7 + 7 = 14	7 + 4 = 11
7 + 10 = 17	7 + 8 = 15	7 + 1 = 8	7 + 2 = 9

2.

Kyle	3	9	7	5	8	4	6
Alex	8	2	4	6	3	7	5

3. a. 8   b. 9   c. 7

4. a. Saturday   b. Tuesday

5. a. There were 25 ants still marching across the yard.
   b. Fourteen students did not arrive late.

Skills Review 31, p. 37

1.

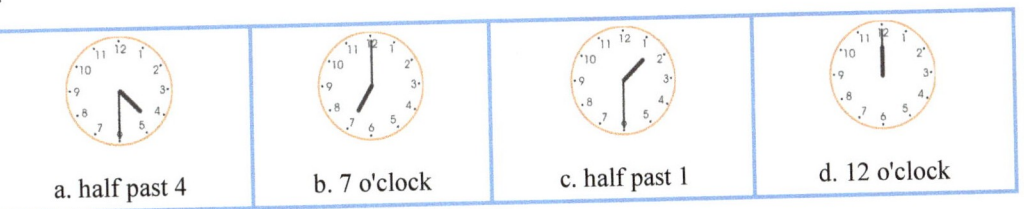

a. half past 4   b. 7 o'clock   c. half past 1   d. 12 o'clock

2. 12, 14, 12, 12, 13, 11

3.

+ 6
4	10
7	13
8	14
10	16

+ 7
3	10
6	13
5	12
7	14

+ 8
2	10
4	12
7	15
8	16

4. a. 72 + 8 = 80   b. 94 + 6 = 100   c. 51 + 9 = 60

Skills Review 32, p. 38

1. 12, 17, 22, 27, 32, 37, 42, 47, 52
   75, 73, 71, 69, 67, 65, 63, 61, 59

2. Her appointment is October 20th. She is going skiing October 24th.

3. a. 50   b. 71   c. 85

4. a. She has 25 pets. Now she has 19 pets.   b. He has 28 cows.

Skills Review 33, p. 39

1.

7	12	2	10	4
16	19	10	14	6
8	11	18	22	16
13	28	20	18	4
10	25	16	12	24
22	31	50	30	32
36	24	39	36	28
42	46	43	40	46
72	41	46	48	42
53	50	48	56	54

2. a. 8   b. 13   c. 4   d. 5   e. 7

3. a. 3   b. 5   c. 2

4. a. Mariah collected one more item.
   b. It took him two and a half hours to put the puzzle together.
      He ate supper at 6:30.

Skills Review 34, p. 40

1.

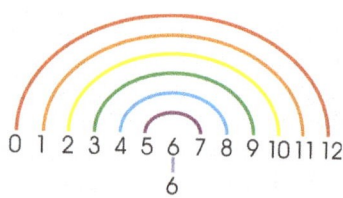

```
12 − 8 = 4        12 − 3 = 9        12 − 4 = 8        12 − 9 = 3
12 − 6 = 6        12 − 10 = 2       12 − 7 = 5        12 − 5 = 7
```

2.

14	20	26	32	38	44	50	56	62	68	74
6	12	18	24	30	36	42	48	54	60	66

3. a. 25 till 9   b. 20 past 11

4.

a. 61 − 8	b. 43 − 7	c. 82 − 9
/ \	/ \	/ \
61 − 1 − 7 = 53	43 − 3 − 4 = 36	82 − 2 − 7 = 73

Chapter 4: Regrouping in Addition

Skills Review 35, p. 41

1. a. 3   b. 6   c. 8   d. 7

2. 12, 9, 7, 15, 16

3. A purple bicycle

4. a. He finished painting the shed at 1:00.
   b. She has $39 left.

Skills Review 36, p. 42

1. a. 73 + 7 = 80   b. 41 + 9 = 50   c. 95 + 5 = 100

2. a. 9   b. 8   c. 9   d. 9   e. 8   f. 9

3. She had to peel 27 potatoes.

4. a. Skippy buried 4 more acorns than Squeaky did.
   b. Squeaky lost 10 of his acorns.

5. Celebration

6. November 9th, November 23rd, December 7th

Skills Review 37, p. 43

1.

2. There are 57 blocks still standing.

3. a. 2:55, 3:05   b. 5:20, 5:30

4. a. 6, 4   b. 9, 4   c. 7, 9

5.

a. 17 + 9 = 26

b. 16 + 15 = 31

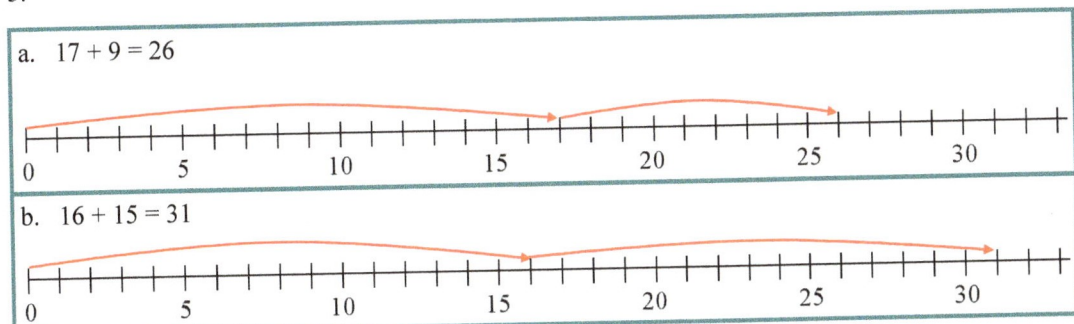

Skills Review 38, p. 44

1. a. 16 < 76   b. 13 < 53

2. a. 1:30, 2:00   b. 5:00, 5:30

3. a. 81 < 83   b. 25 > 22   c. 9 = 9

4. a. Originally, Caleb had 30 hats.
   b. Caleb has 9 hats now.

5.

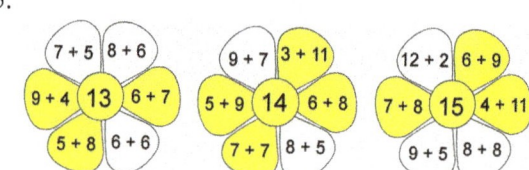

6. a. 3   b. 4

Skills Review 39, p. 45

1. 4 months till July;
   7 months till October;
   9 months till December

2. a. 26   b. 41   c. 85

3.

4.

| a. 17 − 8 = 9 |
| b. 9 + 9 = 18 |
| c. 15 − 7 = 8 |
| d. 6 + 11 = 17 |
| e. 14 − 9 = 5 |
| f. 7 + 9 = 16 |

5. a. The book arrived on Wednesday.
   b. She went to sleep at 11:00. She will have to get up tomorrow morning at 6.

Skills Review 40, p. 46

1.

0 1 2 3 4 5 6 7 8 9 10 11 12 13

13 − 7 = 6   13 − 4 = 9   13 − 9 = 4   13 − 10 = 3
13 − 5 = 8   13 − 6 = 7   13 − 11 = 2   13 − 8 = 5

2.

from	12 midnight	5 AM
to	12 noon	3 PM
hours	12	10

3.

a.   b.   c.

4. a. 51   b. 88   c. 85   d. 95   e. 90

5. He has $35.

Skills Review 41, p. 47

1. August 19th, August 26th, September 2nd

2. a. 86   b. 116   c. 166   d. 157   e. 165

3.

+6, +6, +6, +6, +6, +6, +6, +6

22   28   34   40   46   52   58   64   70

4. a. 24   b. 55   c. 67

5. a. $17 + 30 + 6 = 53$ She has a total of 53 plants   b. $53 - 5 = 48$ Now, she has 48 plants.

Skills Review 42, p. 48

1. a. 56   b. 98   c. 80   d. 99   e. 84

2. a. 9   b. 17   c. 16

3.

Amy	4	(9)	(3)	6	8	(5)	(7)
Kim	10	5	(11)	8	6	(9)	(7)

4. a. 24   b. 46   c. 58

5. a. 8:55, 9:00   b. 7:40, 7:45   c. 6:15, 6:20   d. 8:25, 8:30

Skills Review 43, p. 49

1. a. 6   b. 5   c. 3   d. 2

2. $7 + 9 + 4 = 20$. Each girl got 10 crayons.

3. a. $44 = 44$ b. $31 < 36$ c. $69 > 67$

4. a. $16 + 14 = 30$ b. $12 + 10 = 22$ c. $14 + 13 = 27$

5. a. half past 1   b. 15 till 8   c. 20 past 3

6. a. 34   b. 72   c. 103

Chapter 5: Geometry and Fractions

Skills Review 44, p. 50

1. a. 62 b. 36 c. 71 d. 51 e. 69

2.

50	32	48	26	18
14	24	21	15	20
8	11	12	22	16
13	5	20	6	4
9	25	3	4	24

3. a. 51 + 9 = 60
   b. 63 + 7 = 70
   c. 44 + 6 = 50
   d. 92 + 8 = 100

4. She got 8 more points.

5. a. 12 b. 4 c. 3 d. 4 e. 5 f. 6

Skills Review 45, p. 51

1. a. cow   b. sheep (or lamb)   c. goat   d. frog
2. a. 34   b. 9   c. 55   d. 17   e. 77   f. 27
3. a. half past 1   b. 10 o'clock
4.
   100 − 60 = __40__
   80 − 50 = __30__
   60 − 40 = __20__
   40 − 30 = __10__
   20 − 20 = __0__

5. 8 + 5 + 3 + 6 = 22. He has 22 fruit trees in his orchard.

Skills Review 46, p. 52

1.

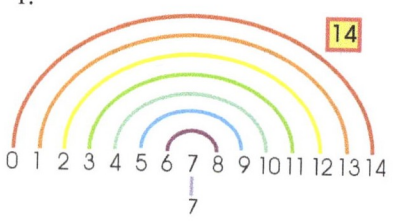

14 − 8 = 6   14 − 3 = 11   14 − 7 = 7   14 − 6 = 8
14 − 5 = 9   14 − 9 = 5   14 − 11 = 3   14 − 4 = 10

2.

3. It took her three hours to do her homework.

4. a. 25   b. 88

Skills Review 47, p. 53

1. a. 74   b. 78   c. 91   d. 89   e. 73

2. Please check the student's work.

3. 14, 16, 18;   64, 90, 120

4. a. 4   b. 6   c. 5

5. a. He went to the water park last Monday.
   b. The difference in price is $6.00.

Skills Review 48, p. 54

1. a. 70   b. 29   c. 50   d. 70

2.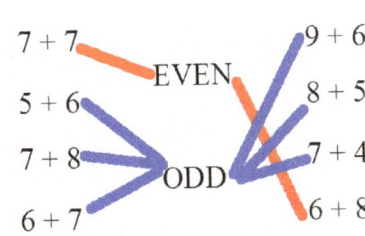

3. Please check the student's work.

4.

5. a. 67 < 71   b. 44 = 44   c. 78 > 77

6. a. He started working at 7:00.   b. Now, he has 35 sheep.

Skills Review 49, p. 55

1. Please check the student's work.

2. a. 34   b. 66   c. 83

3. a. 7   b. 7   c. 5   d. 9

4. Reuben's birthday is September 29th.

5. a. 1:55   b. 10:30   c. 4:45   d. 9:25

6. a. 40   b. 50   c. 30

Skills Review 50, p. 56

1. $27 + $27 + $49 + $49 = $152

2. a. 34   b. 58   c. 82   d. 44   e. 86   f. 27

3. a. Thirty-seven elephants are rolling in the mud now.
   b. Twenty-nine elephants are still rolling in the mud.

4. a. cylinder   b. pyramid   c. cone

5.

11	17	23	29	35	41	47	53	59	65
6	12	18	24	30	36	42	48	54	60

Skills Review 51, p. 57

1. a. 8   b. 6   c. 14   d. 18   e. 17   f. 7
2. a. 25 till 9; 8:35   b. 30 past 1; 1:30
3.

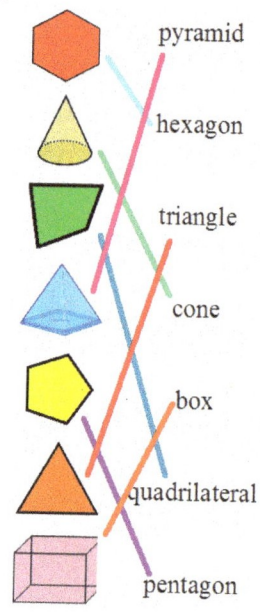

4. a. 19 + 8 = 27   b. 6 + 7 = 13
5.

a.   b.

Chapter 6: Three-Digit Numbers

Skills Review 52, p. 58

1. 12 hours, 16 hours, 6 hours, 7 hours, 17 hours

2. a. 40, 47, 50;   50 is nearer
   b. 80, 83, 90;   80 is nearer
   c. 60, 66, 70;   70 is nearer

3. Please check the student's work.

4. a. Peter jumped rope 12 minutes longer.
   b. The girls dug up a total of 47 potatoes.

Skills Review 53, p. 59

1. Please check the student's work.

2. a. 74   b. 41   c. 80   d. 17   e. 43

3. She found thirty things under her bed.

4. He finished at 4.

5. a. 16 = 8 + 8   b. 80 = 40 + 40   c. 30 = 15 + 15

6.

a.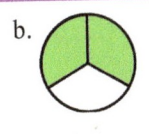

b.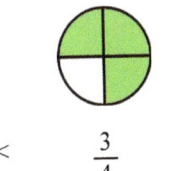

$\frac{2}{3} > \frac{1}{2}$ $\frac{2}{3} < \frac{3}{4}$

Skills Review 54, p. 60

1. 1:55; 2:00

2. 300 + 20 + 2 = 322

3. a. 171   b. 160   c. 91   d. 205   e. 152

4. WOMAN

5. 7, 7, 3
   9, 3, 7
   11, 6, 9
   5, 4, 6

6.

17	26	35	44	53	62	71	80	89	98	107	116
9	18	27	36	45	54	63	72	81	90	99	108

Skills Review 55, p. 61

1. a. Friday   b. Wednesday
2. a. box   b. cylinder   c. cone
3.

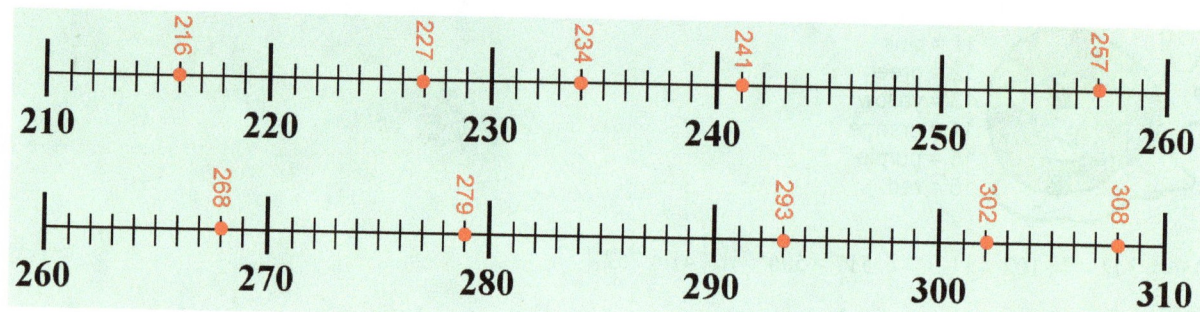

4.

a. 22	b. 50	c. 44
11 + 11 = 22	25 + 25 = 50	22 + 22 = 44
$\frac{1}{2}$ of 22 is 11	$\frac{1}{2}$ of 50 is 25	$\frac{1}{2}$ of 44 is 22.

5. a. She has 32 students this year.   b. There is 5 years difference between the two men's ages.

Skills Review 56, p. 62

1. a. 66 + 5 = 74   b. 17 + 9 = 26   c. 36 + 6 = 42
2. Brett caught Pickles at 2:50.
3. Please check the student's work. You get a pentagon.
4. You get a quadrilateral and a triangle.
5.

+5, +5, +5, +5, +5, +5, +5, +5

37   42   47   52   57   62   67   72   77

6. a. 2/2   b. 1/4   c. 3/4   d. 1/3

Skills Review 57, p. 63

1. a. >   b. =   c. <

2. a. 863   b. 241   c. 476

3.
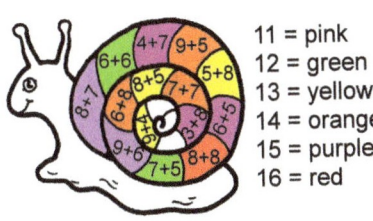

11 = pink
12 = green
13 = yellow
14 = orange
15 = purple
16 = red

4. a. 356 > 342   b. 102 < 112   c. 517 > 506   d. 741 < 752

5. a. △ = 50   b. △ = 90   c. △ = 700

6. a. December   b. Each one got ten crackers.

Skills Review 58, p. 64

1. She will go hiking November 4th, 11th, 18th and 25th.

2. a. 59   b. 52   c. 57   d. 26   e. 29

3. 8 hours; 11 hours

4. Answers will vary, since you can draw the line starting from any vertex. One possibility is shown below.

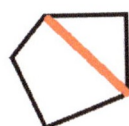

5. a. 4   b. 5   c. 6   d. 7

6.

+	6	8	4	5	7	3	9
6	12	14	10	11	13	9	15
7	13	15	11	12	14	10	16
8	14	16	12	13	15	11	17

Skills Review 59, p. 65

1. a. 715, 725, 735   b. 193, 203, 213

2. a. 27 + 2 = 29
   27 + 4 = 31
   27 + 6 = 33
   27 + 8 = 35
   27 + 10 = 37

3. a. 480   b. 224   c. 336   d. 68

4. a. 15 past 1   b. half past 5   c. 25 till 12

5. a. $65   b. $45   c. $92

Chapter 7: Measuring

Skills Review 60, p. 66

1. a. half past 11   b. 6 o'clock

2. a. 60 + 40 = 100   b. 120 + 80 = 200   c. 580 + 20 = 600   d. 740 + 60 = 800

3. He has 180 more stamps.

4. a. 35   b. 47   c. 18

5. a. 20 < 21   b. 20 > 18

6. Please check the student's work. Answers will vary.

Skills Review 61, p. 67

1. a. 6   b. 5   c. 7   d. 7   e. 5   f. 7

2.

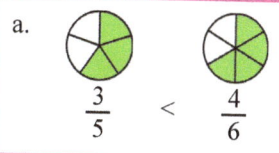 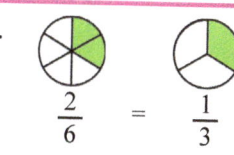

| a. $\frac{3}{5} < \frac{4}{6}$ | b. $\frac{3}{4} > \frac{2}{5}$ | c. $\frac{2}{6} = \frac{1}{3}$ |

3. 1:30   8:05

4. a. 300   b. 200   c. 600

5. Now she has $16.

Puzzle corner:

| 320 + 50 − 20 = 350 | 670 − 50 + 40 − 30 = 630 |
| 790 − 40 + 10 = 760 | 930 − 90 − 20 − 100 = 720 |

Skills Review 62, p. 68

1. a. Six more people went to the library on Friday than Thursday.
   b. There was a total of 38 people.

2. a. 70 = 35 + 35   b. 58 + 29 + 29   c. 66 = 33 + 33

3. a. 71   b. 95   c. 83   d. 83   e. 82

4. Friday, Saturday, Sunday

5. There are 23 muffins left.

Skills Review 63, p. 69

1. a. Shauna baked the fewest. She baked 10 cupcakes.   b. She baked 8 more.   c. They baked a total of 40 cupcakes.

2. a. 410   b. 790   c. 60   d. 199

3. Please check the student's work.

4. a. 30   b. 35   c. 61

Skills Review 64, p. 70

1. a. 30 past 1, 1:30   b. 10 till 6, 5:50   c. 20 past 10, 10:20

2. a. 98   b. 86   c. 82   d. 78   e. 95

3. Please check the student's answers. Answers will vary.

4. a. 100; 300   b. 1,000; 800

Skills Review 65, p. 71

1. The shape is a triangle. Please check the student's answers for the side measurements.

2. a. 26   b. 32   c. 57

3. There are 14 little squares in two-thirds, and 21 squares in the whole rectangle. The rectangle can be divided into thirds either with vertical or horizontal lines.

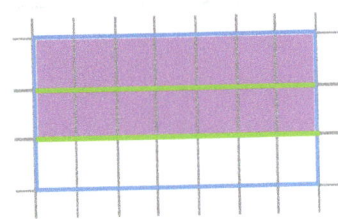

4. a. 6   b. 3   c. 6   d. 9   e. 5   f. 7

5.

22	26	30	34	38	42	46	50	54	58
11	13	15	17	19	21	23	25	27	29

Skills Review 66, p. 72

1.

Distance	Unit
from your wrist to your thumb	in
from your house to the library	mi
the length of your bed	ft in

2.

from	7 AM	12 noon
to	9 PM	2 AM
hours	14	14

3. a. hexagon   b. pyramid, 5 faces   c. cube, six faces   d. quadrilateral

4. a. There were 49 birds.   b. They each got 11 chocolate chips.

Skills Review 67, p. 73

1. Please check the student's work. If more than one finger is the same length, the X should be placed above the other X.

2. a. 236 < 310   b. 127 > 122   c. 574 > 569   d. 736 < 754

3. September 28th, October 12th, October 19th
   April 11th, April 25th, May 2nd

4. She had 57 stickers originally.

5. ODD: 293, 719, 337, 195   EVEN: 102, 348, 186, 152, 544

Chapter 8: Regrouping in Addition and Subtraction

Skills Review 68, p. 74

1. meters, kilometers, centimeters, meters
2. Check the student's work.
3. a. 600   b. 80

4.

6 + 4 = 10	9 + 5 = 14	7 + 8 = 15	9 + 4 = 13
8 + 3 = 11	7 + 6 = 13	9 + 9 = 18	8 + 10 = 18
9 + 7 = 16	9 + 8 = 17	6 + 5 = 11	7 + 7 = 14

5. a. He finished at 1.
   b. She has 200 beads now.

Skills Review 69, p. 75

1. a. 54   b. 42   c. 93   d. 27
2.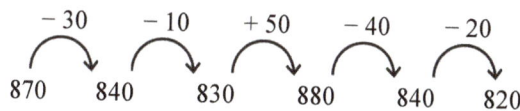
3. Please check the student's answers.
4. a. July   b. December   c. September   d. February
5.
a. 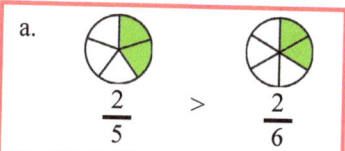 $\frac{2}{5} > \frac{2}{6}$
b. 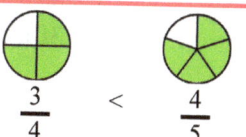 $\frac{3}{4} < \frac{4}{5}$
c. 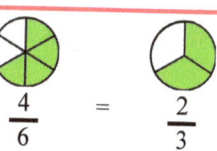 $\frac{4}{6} = \frac{2}{3}$

Skills Review 70, p. 76

1.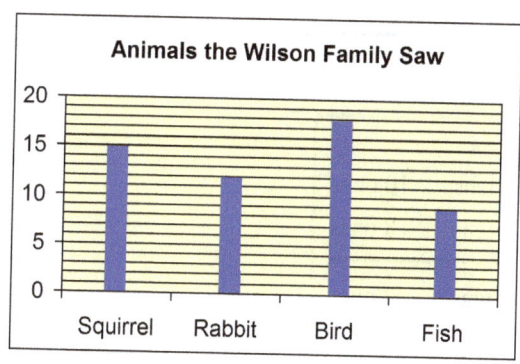
2. a. 130   b. 540   c. 125   d. 507   e. 928
3. Please check the student's work. Answers will vary.
4. He harvested 63 melons.
5.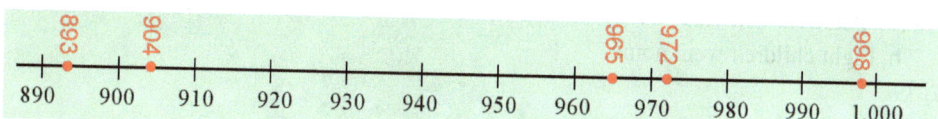

Skills Review 71, p. 77

1. Please check the student's answer. Answers will vary.

2. a. 972   b. 526   c. 921   d. 714

3. a. 458 = 458
   b. 234 < 343
   c. 869 > 795

4. Please check the student's work. Answers will vary.

5. a. 36   b. 37   c. 61

Mystery number: 48

Skills Review 72, p. 78

1.

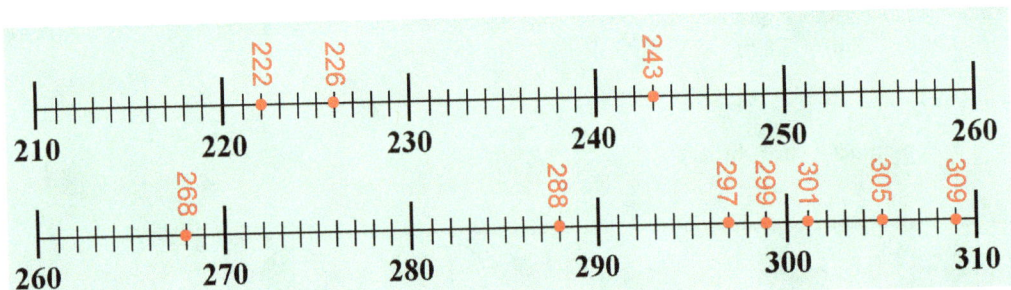

2. a. 112   b. 125   c. 164   d. 115   e. 144

3. Please check the student's answer.

4. a. 20 past 2, 2:20   b. 30 past 4, 4:30   c. 5 till 11, 10:55

Skills Review 73, p. 79

1.

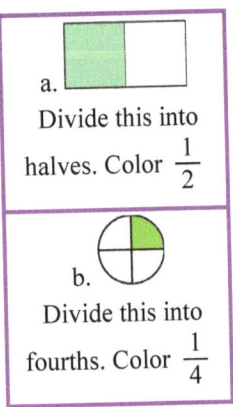

2.

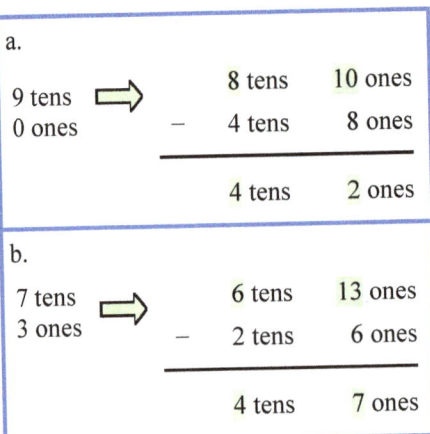

3. Please check the student's answers. Answers will vary.

4. a. Now there are 30 children.   b. Eight children went home.

5. 97, 87, 77, 67, 57, 47, 37, 27, 17

Skills Review 74, p. 80

1. a. 940   b. 355   c. 983

2. a. 33   b. 34

3. He started planting trees at 1:30.

4. a. pentagon   b. pyramid   c. hexagon
   d. triangle   e. cone   f. cylinder

5.

Distance	Unit
from Earth to the moon	mi
the length of a carrot	in
the height of a skyscraper	ft
the distance around a lighthouse	ft

6.

$\frac{1}{2}$ of 14 is 7.

$\frac{1}{2}$ of 22 is 11.

$\frac{1}{2}$ of 50 is 25.

$\frac{1}{2}$ of 48 is 24.

Skills Review 75, p. 81

1. She will play tennis on May 4th, 11th, 18th and 25th.

2. The total cost is $88.

3. a. 139, 142, 234   b. 784, 851, 890

4. $90 - 37 = 53$ $52 - 25 = 27$

5. Please check the student's answers. Answers will vary.

Skills Review 76, p. 82

1.
a. $41 - 1 - 6 = 34$ (−7 branching into 1 and 6)

b. $73 - 3 - 6 = 64$ (−9 branching into 3 and 6)

2.
a. $15 - 8 = 7$
b. $9 + 8 = 17$
c. $16 - 7 = 9$
d. $18 - 9 = 9$

3. Please check the student's work. Answers will vary.

4. a. There are still 18 towels on the line.   b. They have a total of 494 pages.

Chapter 9: Money

Skills Review 77, p. 83

1.

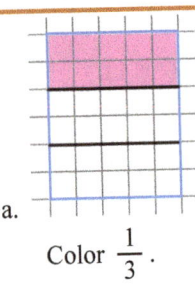
a. Color $\frac{1}{3}$.

10 squares in one third.
30 squares in the whole rectangle.

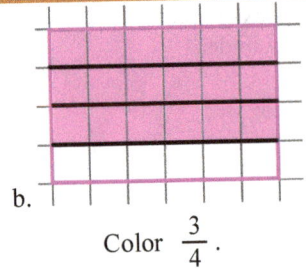
b. Color $\frac{3}{4}$.

18 squares in three fourths.
24 squares in the whole rectangle.

2. Please check the student's work. Answers will vary.

3.

Number	Even?	Odd?	As a double
123		X	
32	X		16 + 16
400	X		200 + 200
91		X	

4. a. 26   b. 22   c. 17   d. 41

Skills Review 78, p. 84

1. a. They sold seven more bottles of orange juice than they sold of the pineapple juice.
   b. Please check the student's work. Answers will vary.

2. a. 36 + 5 = 41   b. 75 + 7 = 82   c. 56 + 8 = 64

3. Each person got 32 cookies.

4. Please check the student's work.
   a. 38¢ = 1 quarter, 1 dime, 3 pennies.
   b. 43¢ = 1 quarter, 1 dime, 1 nickel, 3 pennies.

Skills Review 79, p. 85

1. a. You give 60¢, your change is 5¢.   b. You give 75¢, your change is 7¢.

2. She returned the book on Wednesday.

3. a. 526   b. 546   c. 415

4. a. The fifth duck from the left.
   b. The eighth duck from the right.   b.  a.

Puzzle corner: a. 66 + 18 = 84   b. 57 + 8 = 65   c. 45 + 48 = 93   d. 39 + 19 = 58

Skills Review 80, p. 86

1. a. Aaron picked fifteen pounds fewer apples than Randy picked.
   b. They picked a total of 75 pounds of apples.

2. Answers will vary. Please check the student's work.

3. Please check the student's work. It is a quadrilateral and has four vertices and four sides.

4. They have 183 more miles to travel.

Skills Review 81, p. 87

1. Please check the student's work. Answers will vary.

2. a. 140   b. 110   c. 130

3. 9 hours, 10 hours, 4 hours

4. a. $0.30   b. $0.53

Chapter 10: Exploring Multiplication

Skills Review 82, p. 88

1. a. 5 till 9   b. half past 1   c. 20 past 5

2. a. $1.26   b. $3.85   c. $6.60

3. a. 69; 69 + 29 = 98   b. 36; 36 + 38 = 74   c. 29; 29 + 26 = 55

4. It is a rectangle. Please check the student's answer.

Skills Review 83, p. 89

1. a. 970   b. 845   c. 712

2. a. $7.36   b. $9.39

3. a. 200 lb   b. 2 kg   c. 40 lb or 4 lb, depending on the dog.

4. 100, 97, 94, 91, 88, 85, 82, 79, 76

5. a. 12   b. 15   c. 10

Skills Review 84, p. 90

1. He returned home April 2nd.

2. a. 39 + 4 = 43   b. 66 + 4 = 70   c. 93 + 7 = 100

3. Please check the student's answers. Answers will vary.

4. a. 2 + 2 + 2 + 2 + 2 + 2 + 2 + 2 = 16; 2 × 8 = 16   b. 3 + 3 + 3 + 3 + 3 = 15; 3 × 5 = 15

5. a. $0.21 change. The change can be: 21 pennies; or, four nickels and 1 penny; or, 2 nickels, 1 dime and 1 penny; or, 2 dimes and 1 penny; or, 1 nickel and 16 pennies; or, 1 dime and 11 pennies; or, 2 nickels and 11 pennies; or, 3 nickels and 6 pennies; or, 1 dime, 1 nickel and 6 pennies.

   b. Change is $0.60. The change can be: 2 quarters and 1 dime; or, 6 dimes; or, 1 quarter and 4 dimes and 1 nickel. There are other combinations of coins that can be used. Please check the student's work.

Skills Review 85, p. 91

1. It is a pentagon. Please check the student's answer.

2. $7.18

3. a. 705   b. 332   c. 426   d. 727

4. a.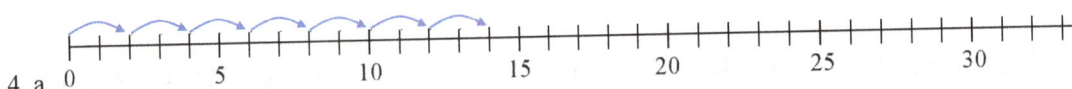

   b.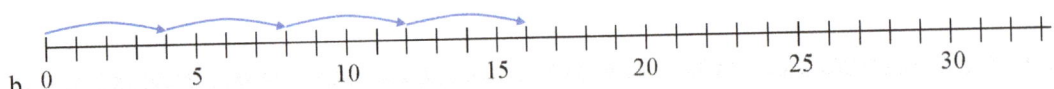

www.ingramcontent.com/pod-product-compliance
Lightning Source LLC
Chambersburg PA
CBHW081025040426
42444CB00014B/3355